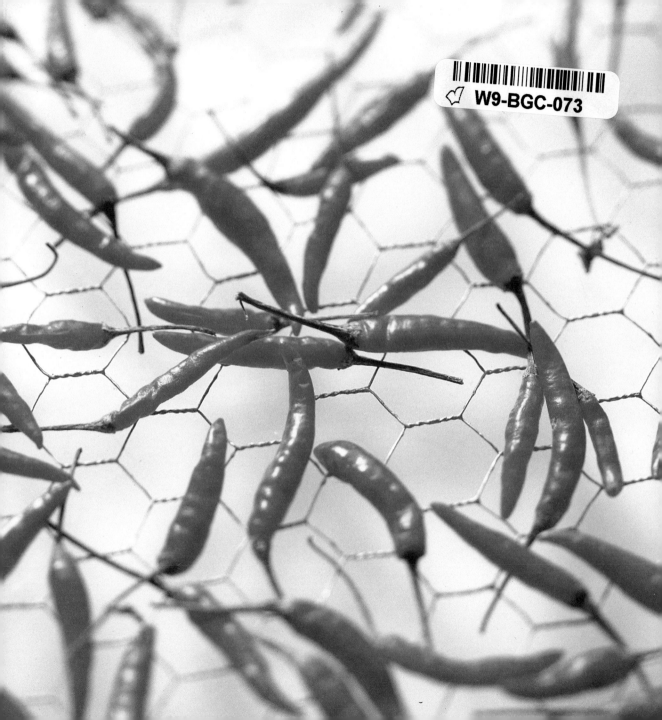

flavouring with Chillies

flavouring with **Chillies**

Clare Gordon-Smith

photography by
James Merrell

RYLAND
PETERS
& SMALL

Art Director **Jacqui Small**

Art Editor **Penny Stock**

Design Assistant **Mark Latter**

Editor **Elsa Petersen-Schepelern**

Photography **James Merrell**

Food Stylist **Clare Gordon-Smith**

Stylist **Sue Skeen**

Production Consultant **Vincent Smith**

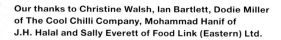

**Our thanks to Christine Walsh, Ian Bartlett, Dodie Miller
of The Cool Chilli Company, Mohammad Hanif of
J.H. Halal and Sally Everett of Food Link (Eastern) Ltd.**

First Published in Great Britain in 1996
by Ryland Peters & Small
Cavendish House, 51–55 Mortimer Street, London W1N 7TD

Text © Clare Gordon-Smith 1996
Design © Ryland Peters & Small 1996

Produced by Mandarin Offset
Printed and bound in China

ISBN 1 900518 01 5

A catalogue of this book is available at the British Library

Notes:
Metric and imperial measurements are
given. Use one set of measurements
only and not a mixture of both.

Ovens should be preheated to the
specified temperature – if using a
fan-assisted oven, adjust time and
temperature according to the
manufacturer's instructions.

Chillies, native to Central and South America, have been enthusiastically adopted by cooks in Europe, Africa, the Middle East, India and South-east Asia, as well as the Americas. Hundreds of different varieties have been identified. Commercially available fresh chillies include, from left, the **Anaheim**, green when unripe and red when ripe, which is widely used in the canning industry and also available fresh. The fiery yellow or red **Jamaican Scotch bonnets** are used in West Indian curries, especially the delectable jerk sauces. Their fruity, smoky flavour is delicious with tropical fruit. The smaller red Jamaican hot chilli is a close relation. Red or green **Thai** and other **Asian** chillies are blazing hot, with a clear fiery taste. Red or green **serrano** chillies are especially suited to roasting, or used fresh in salsas. Yellow, red or orange **habaneros**, closely related to bonnets, are fruity and searingly hot. The mild pale yellow **Caribe** can be used raw in salads. The green **Korean** chilli is as hot as its Thai cousin. Large red or green **New Mexico** chillies, close cousins to the Anaheims, are mild, fleshy and sweet, mostly roasted and used in sauces, salsas and stews.

the flavours of

Chillies

Guajillo
A mild chilli said to taste of 'green tea'. Used in salsas and sauces.

Pasado
*(not illustrated)
Crisp-roasted and skinned – said to taste of apple, celery and citrus.*

Choricero
*(not illustrated)
A very sweet, mild chilli from Spain. This one is large enough to stuff, and can also be added to soups, casseroles and sauces.*

Mulato
Sweet and fruity with a smoky taste–some people can also distinguish the flavour of liquorice. The mulato can be stuffed, or cut into strips and used in Mexican mole dishes.

Cascabel (The Little Rattle)
These pretty little chillies have a nutty taste, thick flesh and medium heat. Soak them first and use in sauces, soups, casseroles and salsas.

New Mexico Red
A very popular large red chilli with an earthy, fruity flavour, good in red sauces.

Tepin Flea Chilli
A small, wild , hand-picked chilli – very hot indeed. Said to taste also of corn and nuts. Usually crushed on to cooked dishes or used to make chilli oils and vinegars.

There are dozens of different kinds of **chillies**, and some have become identified with the cuisines of particular countries. For instance the **fiery** serranos and jalapeños are widely used in Mexico and the United States. Scotch bonnets are identified with Caribbean cooking, while cayenne types are the most popular in India and the Pacific Rim nations of Asia. Native to Mexico, the chilli has been used as food for 7000 years. It was first discovered and taken to Europe after Christopher Columbus's voyage to the New World in 1492, then spread to Europe, Asia, and Africa by the Spaniards and Portuguese.

Nyora
(not illustrated)
Another Spanish chilli with a good, sweet, fruity flavour. It is suitable for use in soups, casseroles and salsas.

Bird's Eye
An orange chilli from East Africa, used in soups and casseroles, chilli oils and vinegars and in Portuguese piri piri sauce.

Guindilla
(not illustrated)
A sweet Spanish chilli with medium heat. It can be used in a wide range of dishes to give extra pizazz.

Pasilla (The Little Raisin)
Used to flavour fish dishes and Mexican moles. Medium hot, it tastes of berries and liquorice.

Habanero
The hottest chilli of all – use it in fish stews, curries and salsas.

Chipotle
(not illustrated)
A very hot but versatile chilli with a delicious, smoky, nutty flavour.

Ancho
(not illustrated)
Sweet, mild and fruity, it can be stuffed, sliced or added to Mexican-style sauces, such as moles. If stuffing, remove the seeds but leave the stems intact.

The chemical that produces their fiery taste is capsaicin. The major part of the chilli's **spicy** heat is in the seeds and membranes, and these should be removed before cooking. When using whole dried chillies, pour over boiling water, soak for about 20 minutes, then remove the stem, core and seeds.

For a nutty taste, dry-roast the dried chillies before using, taking care not to burn them – burnt chillies taste bitter. Capsaicin is not water-soluble, so if your chilli is too hot, don't drink water, beer or wine – milk or yoghurt will quell the fires.

Starters

Thai clear soup
with sweet and sour chilli

A clear Thai soup with chilli as the main
flavouring ingredient. Good chicken stock is
vital too, but if you don't have time to make
your own, you'll find that many supermarkets
now sell freshly made stocks.

If using the Chinese mushrooms, place them in a
small bowl, cover with boiling water and
soak for 30 minutes.
Place the stock, garlic, ginger, rice vinegar and
brown sugar in a pan and heat, stirring constantly,
until gently simmering.
Add the chicken, spring onions, lemongrass, red
chilli and Chinese mushrooms, if using, and continue
to simmer for 15–20 minutes.
Taste and adjust the seasoning, remove the
lemongrass, then serve the soup with
fresh coriander leaves.

3 Chinese mushrooms,
(optional)

900 ml/1½ pints
chicken stock

2 garlic cloves

1 tablespoon sliced
pickled ginger

1½ tablespoons
rice vinegar

2 teaspoons
soft brown sugar

1 chicken breast,
shredded

4 spring onions, sliced

2 stalks lemongrass,
halved lengthways

1 red Thai chilli

salt and freshly
ground black pepper

fresh coriander
leaves, to garnish

Serves 4

Steamed mussels
in a red chilli broth

Use the large, dried red New Mexico
chillies illustrated on page 8. They are
available by mail order if you have difficulty
finding them in specialist shops, or you
could substitute one small dried red chilli
(much hotter than the New Mexico version).
Mussels are naturally inclined to be salty,
so take care when seasoning this recipe.

Roast the garlic and tomatoes in a preheated oven at
150°C (300°F) Gas Mark 2 for 1 hour.
To make the broth, soak the chillies in the stock and
water for about 1 hour until softened and limp.
Purée in a blender and set aside.
Heat 1 tablespoon of the olive oil in a pan and sauté
the garlic and tomato until reheated. Add the
mussels, stir in the broth, cover and steam for about
5–7 minutes until the mussels have opened. Discard
any that remain closed.
Taste and adjust the seasoning, then stir in the
cream, if using, and serve immediately with a
sprinkling of ground paprika, accompanied by
toasted sourdough bread.

2 garlic cloves

4 red tomatoes,
sliced

2 dried red New
Mexico chillies,
stemmed and
deseeded

300 ml/½ pint
fish stock

150 ml/¼ pint water

2 tablespoons olive oil

1 kg/2 lb mussels,
scrubbed and
debearded

150 ml/¼ pint
single cream
(optional)

salt and freshly
ground black pepper

ground paprika,
to serve

Serves 4

Scallop chowder
with Jamaican Scotch bonnets

Chowders are an American contribution to
the culinary repertoire, and the sweet
scallop flavour really comes through in this
version. Jamaican Scotch bonnet chillies are
brilliant red or sunny yellow – and very fiery!
If you can't find Scotch bonnets, use their
close cousins, habaneros, or any other hot,
red, fresh chillies – bonnets are quite large,
so you'll need several smaller ones.
Jamaicans cook them whole in soups and
remove them before serving. The result is
an amazing, spicy, fruity flavour.

Place the scallops in a bowl, sprinkle with lime juice
and set aside for a few minutes.
Brown the bacon in a large, heavy-based pan and
drain off any excess fat. Add the olive oil and, when
hot, add the shallot, celery, garlic and sliced Scotch
bonnet. Sauté gently for a few minutes until lightly
browned, stir in the tomatoes and sherry, then bring
to the boil to burn off the alcohol.
Dice the potatoes and stir into the pan, then add the
herbs and fish stock.
Reserve a few scallops for serving, then chop the
remainder and add to the chowder.
Bring to the boil, simmer for 20 minutes, then
taste and adjust the seasoning.
Add the reserved scallops, sprinkle with parsley and
serve, accompanied by toasted cornbread.

250 g/8 oz scallops

3 tablespoons lime juice

2 rashers unsmoked streaky bacon, chopped

1 tablespoon olive oil

1 shallot, finely chopped

2 celery stalks, finely chopped

2 garlic cloves, crushed

½ red Jamaican Scotch bonnet chilli, deseeded and sliced

3 tomatoes, skinned, deseeded and chopped

2 tablespoons dry sherry

500 g/1 lb potatoes

2 bay leaves

1 bunch of fresh, flat leaf parsley, chopped, plus 4 tablespoons, to serve

600 ml/1 pint fish stock

salt and pepper

Serves 4

Roasted chilli soup
with yellow and red peppers

This vibrantly coloured soup has a bright zip
of chilli coming through the tons of tomato
and pepper flavour. Serve hot or chilled.

Place the red and yellow peppers and the red chilli
under a very hot grill and roast on all sides until the
skins are blackened and blistered. Wrap in clingfilm
and leave to steam for 5–7 minutes. Pull out the
stems and seeds, scrape off the skin and discard.
Slice the flesh into strips and reserve the
yellow pepper for garnish.
Heat the oil in a large, heavy-based pan, add the
shallot or onion, the tomatoes, chilli and red
peppers, replace the lid and cook the vegetables for
about 5 minutes until softened. Stir in the stock and
seasoning and simmer for 20 minutes until all the
vegetables are tender. Place in a blender or food
processor and purée until smooth.
Reheat, taste and adjust the seasoning.
Serve garnished with the strips of yellow pepper and
a drizzle of chilli oil, accompanied by the croûtons
and crème fraîche.

2 red peppers

1 red serrano chilli

1 tablespoon sunflower
oil, or other mild oil

1 shallot or small onion,
finely chopped

500 g/1 lb ripe
red plum tomatoes,
skinned and deseeded

600 ml/1 pint
vegetable stock

salt and freshly
ground black pepper

to serve

1 yellow pepper

chilli oil, to taste

croûtons

4 tablespoons
crème fraîche

Serves 4

Chilli aïoli
with char-grilled vegetables

Aïoli is the wonderful garlic mayonnaise from
Provence, served with steamed vegetables
and salt cod or other poached fish. Make it
with chillies, and serve it with char-grilled
vegetables, and the whole dish becomes
even more vibrant and sun-drenched!

To prepare the vegetables, first par-boil the
artichokes, then drain.
Brush all the vegetables with olive oil, sprinkle with
sea salt and cook under a very hot grill, or on a
cast-iron grill pan, until browned.
To make the aïoli, first place the chilli under the grill
and roast until the skin is blistered and browned.
Pull out and discard the stem and seeds, then mash
the flesh. Place the garlic, egg yolks, breadcrumbs,
chilli, salt and vinegar in a food processor and purée
to a paste. With the motor running, pour in the olive
oil in a thin stream until the mixture forms a thick
sauce. Thin with a little boiling water if necessary.
Serve as a dip with the roasted vegetables or, as
an alternative, with raw crudités.

a selection of
vegetables, such as
baby artichokes,
asparagus, fennel,
leeks or peppers

olive oil, for brushing

sea salt

chilli aïoli

1 red habanero chilli

2 garlic cloves, crushed

2 egg yolks

3 tablespoons fresh
white breadcrumbs

4 tablespoons
white wine vinegar

300 ml/½ pint olive oil

1 tablespoon boiling
water (optional)

pinch of salt

Serves 4

Chilli-stuffed squid
with rocket and chilli oil

Baby squid are delicious stuffed with a
mixture of sweet brióche crumbs, chillies
and serrano ham – a zingy starter, and
wonderful as a main course for lunch, served
with rice or couscous. If you don't have a
cast-iron grill pan, you could also cook the
squid on a barbecue, or roast in a hot oven
at 200°C (400°F) Gas Mark 6 for 10 minutes.

To make the stuffing, melt the butter in a frying pan
and when sizzling, add the brióche crumbs and fry
until golden. Remove from the pan, place in a bowl
and mix in the remaining stuffing ingredients.
To prepare the squid, gently pull the body away from
the head and tentacles, then cut off the tentacles
and reserve. Rinse out the bodies and discard the
transparent quill and the head.
Place the stuffing mixture loosely in the squid bodies
and fasten shut using soaked wooden cocktail
sticks. Brush the bodies with olive oil and season
with salt and freshly ground black pepper.
Heat an oiled cast-iron grill pan on top of the stove,
and sear the stuffed squid and tentacles for about
5 minutes on each side.
To serve, arrange the rocket or mustard leaves on
serving plates, and place the squid on top.
Drizzle with chilli oil and serve immediately.

8 squid

olive oil, for brushing

salt and freshly
ground black pepper

chilli stuffing

25 g/1 oz butter

50 g/2 oz briôche
breadcrumbs

1 tablespoon
finely chopped
fresh coriander leaves

1 garlic clove, crushed

1 green habanero chilli,
finely chopped

2 slices serrano ham,
finely chopped

grated rind and
juice of 1 lime

salt and freshly
ground black pepper

to serve

250 g/8 oz rocket or
mustard leaves

chilli oil

Serves 4

n easy, stunning dish with a **mild** chilli flavour

Crab cushions
with chilli dipping sauce

A hip-hot starter. You can buy chilli dipping
sauce, or make your own. Deseed and chop
1 red chilli and mix with 6 tablespoons rice
vinegar and 2 tablespoons tomato ketchup.

6 sheets ricepaper

oil, for deep-frying

125 ml/4 fl oz chilli
dipping sauce
(see introduction)

crab filling

2 green Thai chillies

3 spring onions

1 bunch of coriander

4 Chinese mushrooms

50 g/2 oz
transparent noodles

175 g/6 oz
white crabmeat

2 teaspoons soy sauce

1 tablespoon fish sauce

Serves 4

Mix all the chilli dipping sauce ingredients together,
place in a small bowl and set aside.
To make the filling, deseed and chop the chillies,
then finely chop the spring onions and coriander.
Soak the mushrooms and noodles separately in warm
water for 10 minutes, then drain and discard the
soaking water. Mix all the filling ingredients.
To make the cushions, soak the ricepaper in warm
water until soft, spoon a small amount of filling into
the centre of each sheet and fold into parcels. Cover
with a damp cloth to prevent them drying out.
Heat the oil in a frying pan and deep-fry the parcels
for a few minutes, until pale gold and crispy.
Serve immediately with the chilli dipping sauce.

a hip-hot **partnership** – chillies and

crab are one of the great combinations

Crab cakes
with sweet red pepper sauce

Crab cakes make great starters – and are excellent party food. Chilli and crab seem just made for each other! Use one small red chilli if you can't find jalapeños.

Mix the breadcrumbs, egg, crabmeat, jalapeño chillies, coriander, salt and freshly ground black pepper in a bowl. Cover and set aside.

To make the sauce, peel the peppers with a vegetable peeler, cut in half, deseed and roughly chop. Deseed and chop the red chilli. Place in a saucepan with the shallots, thyme, garlic, peppercorns and tomato. Add the stock, bring to the boil and simmer until soft. Add the white vermouth and vinegar, bring to the boil and reduce for 3–4 minutes. Place in a blender or food processor and purée until smooth. Return to the pan, reheat and simmer gently until ready to serve.

To cook the crab cakes, heat the oil in a large frying pan until hot but not smoking. Add spoonfuls of the mixture and fry for a few minutes on each side until golden. Drain on kitchen paper.

Serve with the hot red pepper sauce. A few green salad leaves would be a suitable accompaniment.

125 g/4 oz dried breadcrumbs

1 egg, lightly beaten

500 g/1 lb crabmeat

1–2 jalapeño chillies, deseeded and diced

1 bunch of coriander, roughly chopped

salt and pepper

groundnut oil, for frying

red pepper sauce

2 red peppers

1 small red chilli

2 shallots, sliced

1 sprig of thyme

1 garlic clove, crushed

10 black peppercorns

1 plum tomato, sliced

250 ml/8 fl oz vegetable stock

4 tablespoons white vermouth

1 tablespoon white wine vinegar

Serves 4

Main courses

Thai seafood curry
with coriander and coconut milk

Thai fish curries taste clean and fresh, and are absolutely packed with spicy flavour. It's important not to overcook the seafood, so remove it from the broth as soon as it is cooked, then reheat just before serving.

Pour the coconut milk into a pan, add the chillies and lemongrass and bring to the boil. Add the mussels and remove as soon as they open. Add the pieces of monkfish and the tiger prawns and poach gently until the prawns change colour and the fish becomes opaque. Remove from the pan and set aside with the mussels. Return the coconut milk to the boil and reduce by half. Return the seafood to the pan and reheat, then serve with fragrant Thai rice or pasta, scattered with torn coriander leaves.

300 ml/½ pint coconut milk

1 red Thai chilli, deseeded and sliced

1 green Thai chilli, deseeded and sliced

2 stalks of lemongrass, cut in half lengthways

500 g/1 lb mussels, scrubbed and debearded

500 g/1 lb cod or monkfish tail

500 g/1 lb tiger prawns, shelled and deveined

leaves from 1 bunch of coriander, torn

fragrant Thai rice, or pasta, to serve

Serves 4

Prawn brochettes
with chilli, papaya and mango salsa

You can adapt this recipe for the barbecue –
the woodsmoke adds a marvellous depth of
flavour. Always cook the prawns with their
shells on, again for extra flavour.

To make the salsa, mix the ingredients together in a
small container, cover and chill for up to 6 hours.
Place the prawns in a bowl, sprinkle over the chilli
oil and the juice of 2 limes. Marinate for 1–2 hours.
Soak 4 wooden skewers in water for 30 minutes.
Place a wedge of red onion on each skewer, then
thread on the prawns, followed by a slice of lime.
Brush with the marinade, sprinkle with sea salt,
then cook under a preheated grill for a few
minutes on each side.
Serve, garnished with wedges of lime and onion, the
sliced chilli and torn coriander leaves, together with
the salsa spooned over or served separately.
Rice, pita bread or salad would be
suitable accompaniments.

salsas are thick and chunky sauces – ideal made wi

fresh fruit. This one is also wonderf

opped

ade with grapes.

24 unshelled prawns

1 teaspoon chilli oil

juice of 4 limes, plus
1 lime, sliced, and
1 lime, quartered

1 large red onion,
cut into 8 wedges

sea salt

chilli, papaya
and mango salsa

1 large, ripe mango,
peeled, deseeded
and diced

1 ripe papaya, about
250 g/8 oz, peeled,
deseeded and diced

. 1 tablespoon
balsamic vinegar

1 tablespoon chopped
fresh red chillies

salt and freshly
ground black pepper

to serve

1 fresh red chilli, sliced

fresh coriander leaves

Serves 4

Pork tenderloin
with red apple chilli chutney

This sparkling fresh chutney of apples and chilli, with just a hint of vinegar, is a terrific new approach to the traditional apple sauce. If you can't find habanero chillies, use a Scotch bonnet or two small Asian chillies.

Mix the marinade ingredients together. Trim any fat from the pork, place the fillet in a flat dish, pour over the marinade, cover with clingfilm and set aside in the refrigerator for at least 1 hour, or overnight. When ready to cook, remove the meat from the marinade, pat dry with kitchen paper, and place in a roasting tin. Roast in a preheated oven at 200°C (400°F) Gas Mark 6 for 20–30 minutes, until well cooked. Remove from the pan and rest in a warm place for about 5 minutes.

Meanwhile, to make the chutney, heat the oil in a shallow frying pan, add the shallot and cook until soft and golden. Chop the apple, add to the pan, and stir. Add the remaining ingredients and the marinade juices, stir well, bring to the boil and simmer for 15 minutes.

Cut the pork into slices and serve with the apple and chilli chutney. Pappardelle or other pasta tossed in extra-virgin olive oil and the green chilli paste on page 61 are suitable accompaniments.

500 g/1 lb pork fillet

orange marinade

grated rind and juice of 2 oranges

1 teaspoon lemon juice

1 garlic clove, crushed

1 teaspoon soy sauce

1–2 teaspoons chilli powder

1 teaspoon soft brown sugar

red apple chilli chutney

2 teaspoons chilli oil

1 shallot or small onion, finely chopped

2 Cox's apples

1 red habanero chilli, deseeded and chopped

2 tablespoons sherry vinegar

pinch of sea salt

Serves 4

Garlic ginger chicken
with raspberry harissa

A recipe created by talented London designer Dinny Hall – and very stylish it is too! Cook in a roasting tin, or in a chicken brick, with enough chicken stock added to fill the brick to about 5 cm/2 inches deep.

Pierce the skin of the chicken at regular intervals and insert small pieces of garlic and ginger. Brush the chicken with a little chilli oil and place in a roasting tin (or soaked chicken brick with chicken stock added). Cook in a preheated oven at 200°C (400°F) Gas Mark 6 for about 1½ hours, until tender.

To make the harissa, heat the olive oil, add the chopped onions and fry until golden. Add the garlic, mustard seeds, bay leaf, chilli powder, salt and vinegar and cook gently until the mixture is soft and golden. Add the tomatoes and raspberries, bring to the boil and simmer on a low heat for 1 hour. Remove and discard the bay leaf, pour into a blender or food processor and purée until smooth.

Remove the chicken from the oven and serve accompanied by the harissa and couscous. The couscous can be served plain, or spiced with chilli oil, cinnamon, garlic and vanilla.

1 free-range chicken,
about 2 kg/4 lb

2 garlic cloves, sliced

2.5 cm/1 inch piece of
fresh ginger, sliced

2 teaspoons chilli oil

chicken stock
(see method)

couscous, to serve

raspberry harissa

2 tablespoons olive oil

2 red onions,
finely chopped

1 garlic clove, crushed

1 teaspoon mustard
seeds, lightly crushed

1 bay leaf

1 teaspoon chilli
powder, or to taste

1 tablespoon vinegar

250 g/8 oz
tomatoes, skinned

250 g/8 oz raspberries

salt

Serves 4

Main courses **33**

Chicken and chorizo
in a chilli and orange sauce

An easy, spicy, one-pot dish. Pretty red
Camargue rice from France has a nutty
flavour, but you could use basmati instead.

500 g/1 lb potatoes

4 plum tomatoes

2 tablespoons olive oil

250 g/8 oz baby onions

2 whole garlic cloves

4 chicken breasts

2 chorizo sausages

2 tablespoons harissa
or hot chilli paste

pinch of chilli powder

3 tablespoons sherry

grated rind and juice
of 1 large orange

salt and pepper

to serve

toasted cumin seeds

soured cream

Serves 4

Peel the potatoes and cut into chunks, then skin and
chop the tomatoes. Heat the oil in a large frying pan,
add the potatoes and onions and sauté for about
10 minutes, then add the garlic and fry until golden.
Cut the chicken breasts into 5 cm/2 inch pieces and
thickly slice the chorizos, then stir into the potato
and onion mixture. Stir in the chopped tomatoes,
harissa, chilli powder, sherry, orange rind and juice.
Taste and adjust the seasoning, then simmer for
15 minutes, until the chicken is tender.
Sprinkle with toasted cumin seeds and serve with a
dollop of soured cream.
Steamed red Camargue rice, and a crisp green salad
are suitable accompaniments.

Marinated duck breasts
with orange salsa and sherry sauce

A Pan-Pacific recipe, combining the culinary traditions of Asia and Mexico. The chilli flavouring in the marinade comes from Tabasco sauce, made in Louisiana since the middle of last century, from chillies which originated in the Mexican state of Tabasco.

Score the duck skin in a criss-cross pattern to help the fat melt off during cooking. Place the breasts in a roasting tin with the skin side up.
Mix the marinade ingredients together, pour over the duck and set aside for at least 30 minutes.
Meanwhile, to make the salsa, mix all the ingredients together and chill until ready to serve.
Baste the duck breasts with the marinade, then place the roasting tin in a preheated oven at 200°C (400°F) Gas Mark 6 for about 20 minutes or until the breasts are just pink. Remove the breasts and keep warm.
Drain the fat from the roasting tin, add the sherry, bring to the boil to remove the alcohol, then stir in the stock and simmer for 5 minutes.
Slice the duck breasts and serve with the sherry sauce and orange salsa, accompanied by stir-fried cabbage.

2 large duck breasts

honey marinade

1 tablespoon sesame oil

2 tablespoons soy sauce

1 tablespoon honey

1 teaspoon Tabasco sauce

orange salsa

1 shallot or small onion, finely chopped

2 oranges, segmented

1 yellow Scotch bonnet chilli, deseeded and finely chopped

1 bunch of basil, roughly torn

1 small red pepper, deseeded and finely chopped

sherry sauce

2 tablespoons dry sherry

150 ml/¼ pint vegetable stock

Serves 4

Harissa honey quail
roasted with sweet potatoes

Harissa paste is one of the great ingredients of North African and Middle Eastern cooking, and often served with dishes accompanied by couscous. It can be bought ready-made, but it is easy to make yourself – just soak 25 g/1 oz dried chillies in warm water for 1 hour. Drain and purée with 2 tablespoons fresh coriander, 1 tablespoon fresh mint, a pinch of salt, a garlic clove, and enough oil to give a thick paste.

Mix the harissa coating ingredients together, then spread on to the quail, place in a roasting tin and cook in a preheated oven at 200°C (400°F) Gas Mark 6 for about 20 minutes, or until done. (The birds are cooked when a skewer inserted into the thickest part of the thigh produces clear juices with no trace of pink.)
Set aside to rest for 10 minutes before serving. Cut the sweet potatoes into thick chunks, brush them with a little olive oil, sprinkle with sea salt, place in another roasting tin and cook at the same temperature for 20 minutes.
Serve the quail with the sweet potatoes. A steamed green vegetable would be a suitable accompaniment.

4 quail

375 g/12 oz sweet potatoes

2 teaspoons olive oil

sea salt

sherry, honey and harissa coating

3 tablespoons honey

2 tablespoons dry sherry

2 tablespoons harissa paste

salt

Serves 4

Pan-fried venison
with chilli and pear sauce

This delicious combination of fruit and meat
is typical of Middle Eastern and medieval
cookery. Add a dash of chilli and soy sauce
for an East-meets-West flavour. You could
use venison sausages instead of venison for
a more homely version of this recipe.

Heat the butter and olive oil in a large frying pan,
add the venison and gently sauté for a few minutes
until brown. Remove from the pan and set aside to
rest in a warm place.
Add the sliced pears to the pan, sprinkle with the
sugar, then gently sauté until lightly golden.
Add the red wine, soy sauce, chilli and cornflour
mixture, bring to the boil and simmer for 5 minutes.
Serve the venison steaks with the sauce poured
around, accompanied by steaming roast potatoes
and shredded cabbage sautéed with caraway seeds.
Alternatively, return the venison steaks to the sauce
and simmer gently for 3 minutes before serving.

an unusual **sweet and spicy** dish with

just a hint of chilli heat

25 g/1 oz butter

1 tablespoon olive oil

500 g/1 lb venison
fillet, cut into
2.5 cm/1 inch steaks

2 pears, peeled,
quartered and sliced

½ teaspoon sugar

175 ml/6 fl oz red wine

1 tablespoon
light soy sauce

1 red chilli, roasted

1 tablespoon
cornflour, mixed
with 2 tablespoons
cold water

Serves 4

Vegetables

Corn crêpes with
chilli vegetables and tomato salsa

These pretty yellow pancakes, made with polenta, have a sweet, nutty texture. Add a dollop of soured cream and this dish could be served by itself for lunch, or as a starter – or as a sumptuous treat for vegetarians.

To make the crêpes, place the polenta grain, plain flour and salt in a bowl, then beat in the eggs and milk to form a smooth batter. Set aside.

To make the filling, crush the garlic, slice the onions and cut the squash in quarters. Core, deseed and chop the red peppers and pickled chilli. Heat the oil in a pan, add the garlic, onions, squash, peppers, chilli and salt, and fry gently until tender.

To make the salsa, roughly chop the tomatoes and finely chop the spring onions. Deseed and roughly chop the red chilli, then mix all the ingredients together and chill until ready to use.

To cook the crêpes, heat the oil in an 18 cm/7 inch frying pan. Add a ladle of batter and swirl the pan around so the mixture covers the base. Cook until the surface bubbles and the base is browned, then turn and brown the other side. Remove and set aside in a warm place while you cook the remaining crêpes. Spoon the filling into the crêpes and serve with the tomato salsa.

50 g/2 oz polenta grain

50 g/2 oz plain flour

pinch of salt

3 eggs

200 ml/7 fl oz semi-skimmed milk

2 garlic cloves

2 red onions

12 patty pan squash

2 red peppers

1 pickled red jalapeño chilli

1 tablespoon olive oil

pinch of salt

1 bunch of coriander

oil, for deep-frying

tomato salsa

4 ripe tomatoes

2 spring onions

1 red chilli

2 tablespoons red wine vinegar

Serves 4

Spinach dhaal
with toasted coconut

Lentils are a good source of protein for vegetarians and they work well as a base for hot chillies. In India, dhaal is a traditional accompaniment to rice, flat breads and curried vegetables, meats or poultry.

Place the lentils in a pan, add the turmeric and about 1.2 litres/2 pints water. Bring to the boil, then cover with the lid slightly ajar. Reduce the heat and simmer for about 20 minutes, then add salt and cook for about 15—20 minutes more, until the lentils are cooked and tender, and have absorbed all the liquid. Heat the oil in a small frying pan until very hot, add the spices and gently fry to release the aromas, then add the spinach and gently sauté for a few minutes until the leaves turn bright green. Heap the spiced spinach on heated plates and spoon the yellow dhaal beside. Sprinkle with shredded or toasted coconut, if using, and serve.

375 g/12 oz
yellow split peas
(channa dhaal), washed

½ teaspoon
ground turmeric

3 tablespoons
vegetable oil

1 teaspoon salt

1 teaspoon cumin seeds

1 cinnamon stick

3–5 dried, hot
red chillies

250 g/8 oz fresh
spinach leaves

2 tablespoons
shredded coconut,
or coconut flakes,
toasted (optional)

Serves 4

a **spicy trea**t for vegetarians—and great wi

eat and poultry

Provençal ragoût
of tomatoes, fennel and potato

A mild chilli dish with just a hint of fire –
great for people with sensitive palates.

500 g/1 lb tomatoes

2 fennel bulbs

4 shallots

500 g/1 lb new
potatoes, unpeeled

2 garlic cloves, crushed

1 red pepper

2 teaspoons harissa
paste (see page 39)

strip of orange peel

1 bay leaf

150 ml/¼ pint
vegetable stock

2 tablespoons
sun-dried tomato pesto

2 red serrano chillies

salt and pepper

Serves 4

Skin and quarter the tomatoes, trim and slice the
fennel and cut the shallots into quarters.
Place all the ingredients, except the sun-dried
tomato pesto and chillies, into a saucepan, bring to
the boil and simmer for 25 minutes.
Roast or grill the serrano chillies, then remove the
seeds and membranes. Chop the chillies and mix
with the sun-dried tomato pesto, stir into the stew
and serve with crusty bread.
As an alternative for those who love a fiery chilli
flavour, you could substitute red habanero or
Scotch bonnet chillies.

Caribbean curry

A mixture of pumpkin, plantains, peppers and peas simmered in a chilli and coconut stock and served with spiced rice – fry 1 teaspoon each of cinnamon, chopped ginger and cumin seeds in 1 tablespoon of sunflower oil, then stir through plain boiled or steamed rice. If you can't easily find plantains, use bananas instead.

To prepare the butternut squash, cut in half, remove and discard the seeds, peel off the skin and cut the flesh into chunky cubes.

Heat the chilli oil in a heavy-based pan, add the sliced chillies, cinnamon sticks and cloves and let them sizzle to release their aromas.

Stir in the chopped onion and cook until softened and a little golden. Stir in the squash and plantain, add the vegetable stock and coconut milk, bring to the boil and simmer for 10 minutes.

Add the lemon juice, green pepper and peas, cook for a further 10 minutes and serve. Steaming spiced rice would be a suitable accompaniment.

2 butternut squash

1 tablespoon chilli oil

2 red chillies, deseeded and sliced

2 cinnamon sticks

6 cloves

1 onion, roughly chopped

1 plantain, peeled and thickly sliced

300 ml/½ pint vegetable stock

150 ml/¼ pint coconut milk

1 teaspoon fresh lemon juice

1 green pepper, cored, deseeded and cut into chunks

125 g/4 oz fresh or frozen peas

Serves 4

Rice noodles
with green papaya and mooli

Noodles in a light sweet and sour sauce is
a dish that's rapidly becoming the stir-fry
of the nineties. This dish makes a fresh
summer starter – and is also good as an
accompaniment for main dishes such as
char-grilled beef fillet.

To make the chilli dressing, mix together the lime
juice, fish sauce, palm sugar, chillies, lime leaves,
red shallots and lemongrass. Set aside.
Cut the rice noodles into 15 cm/6 inch strips, place
in a colander, pour over a kettle of boiling water and
set aside. Peel and deseed the papaya and cut into a
fine julienne. Peel and slice the mooli.
Drain the softened noodles and place in a bowl.
When cool, stir in the papaya, mooli, strips of chilli.
orange segments and the dressing, then serve,
garnished with mint leaves.

250 g/8 oz rice noodles

1 green papaya

1 mooli or daikon
(Japanese radish)

2 red New Mexico
chillies, cored,
deseeded and
cut into strips

1 orange, segmented

sprigs of mint leaves

chilli dressing

juice of 3 limes

4 tablespoons *nam pla*
(Thai fish sauce)

4 teaspoons palm sugar

4 green chillies,
deseeded and
finely sliced

4 small kaffir lime
leaves, finely shredded

4 red shallots, chopped

3 stalks lemongrass,
thinly sliced

Serves 4

a modern update on a Thai recipe

with **five stars** on the chilli heat scale

Vegetable fritters
with coriander chilli mint raita

Wonderful as party food, these light fritters
will also make perfect starters. Vary the
vegetables to suit yourself, and serve with
this wonderful raita with a hint of chilli.

To make the raita, roughly chop the mint and
coriander, and place in a mixing bowl. Deseed and
chop the chillies. Peel and finely chop the ginger.
Add to the bowl with the garlic. Add the grated zest
and juice of the limes, together with the salt and
yoghurt. Chill until ready to serve.
To make the batter, first chop the coriander and
mint, then place in a bowl with the flour, turmeric,
and sugar. Whisk the egg white until stiff, carefully
fold in the spiced flour, stir in the lime juice and
enough water to give a light batter.
Break the cauliflower into florets, cut the courgettes
into 2.5 cm/1 inch slices and trim the carrots.
Heat vegetable oil in a deep-fryer or saucepan.
Dip each piece of vegetable into the batter and
deep-fry in hot oil until golden brown. Drain on
kitchen paper. Serve hot with the raita.

4 sprigs of coriander

4 sprigs of mint

75 g/3 oz gram flour

pinch of turmeric

pinch of sugar

1 egg white

juice of 1 lime

pinch of salt

250 g/8 oz cauliflower

175 g/6 oz courgettes

1 bunch of baby carrots

oil, for deep-frying

chilli mint raita

4 sprigs of mint

4 sprigs of coriander

2 green chillies

1 cm/½ inch piece of
fresh ginger

1 garlic clove, crushed

2 limes

pinch of sea salt

4 tablespoons yoghurt

Serves 4

Vegetable patties
with spicy tomato chutney

These vegetarian patties are made from a base of sweet potato with the addition of grated courgettes and grated carrots.

625 g/1¼ lb sweet potatoes

375 g/12 oz courgettes

200 g/7 oz carrots

1 green Asian chilli

1 spring onion

2 tablespoons yoghurt

salt and black pepper

vegetable oil, for frying

spicy tomato chutney

4 tomatoes

1–2 red chillies

2 tablespoons chopped fresh mint

1 tablespoon cider vinegar

pinch of sea salt

Serves 4

To make the chutney, roughly chop the tomatoes, finely chop the chillies, then mix with the mint, vinegar and salt. Set aside until ready to serve. To make the patties, first boil and mash the sweet potatoes. Grate the courgettes, sprinkle with salt and set aside for 30 minutes to draw out some of the juices. Drain and pat dry. Grate the carrots, deseed and chop the chilli and slice the spring onion. Mix the vegetables, yoghurt, salt and pepper in a bowl. With floured hands, shape the mixture into 8 patties. Heat a shallow layer of oil in a heavy-based pan and fry the patties for 4 minutes on both sides. Serve immediately with the spicy tomato chutney.

Red pepper compote
with feta cheese

6 red peppers

2 red habanero or
Scotch bonnet chillies

125 g/4 oz feta cheese

2 garlic cloves, crushed

250 ml/½ pint olive oil

salt

Serves 4

Olive oil is a great combo with chillies.

Roast, skin, deseed and quarter the peppers and chillies. Place a layer of peppers in a bowl, then a layer of feta. Season, add half the garlic and half a chilli, then pour over some olive oil. Repeat until all ingredients have been used. Chill for 24 hours before serving with warmed bread and a selection of salads.

Chilli parsley pesto
for pasta and steamed vegetables

250 g/8 oz leeks

250 g/8 oz broccoli

500 g/1 lb dried pasta

chilli pesto

3 tablespoons pine nuts

3 green Caribe chillies

1 small garlic clove

4 tablespoons olive oil

juice of 1 lime

1 bunch flat leaf parsley

sea salt, to taste

Serves 4

An especially zippy pesto – great with pasta,
and terrific with bruschetta too.

To make the pesto, roast and skin the chillies and roast the pine nuts. Place all the ingredients in a blender or food processor and purée until smooth. Set aside until ready to use.
Trim and slice the leeks and cut the broccoli into florets. Cook the pasta in a pan of boiling salted water until just tender, and steam the vegetables. To serve, drain the pasta, place in a serving bowl or 4 heated pasta plates, stir in about 4 tablespoons of pesto, and pile the vegetables on top.

Accompaniments

Above, from left, Green chilli paste (recipe
page 61), Cucumber chilli chutney (page 60)
and Avocado relish (page 61).

Chilli vodka

There are many wonderfully flavoured vodkas – and parties to match! Your own fiery chilli vodka will be a great talking point.

Add the chillies to the vodka and leave to marinate for 1–2 days, according to taste. Remove the chillies, keep the bottle in the freezer and serve after dinner or as a nightcap after dancing the night away.

1 bottle vodka

2 big red chillies or 4 smaller ones, halved lengthways

Makes 1 bottle

Chilli chutney
with grapefruit and cucumber

This is an instant chutney best made and served within a few days. It is ideal for those lazy summer days full of convivial barbecue parties and general *al fresco* eating. Serve it with home-made burgers or sausages.

Peel the cucumbers, scoop out the seeds, slice, sprinkle over half the salt and leave to marinate while you prepare the remaining ingredients. Roughly chop the pickled dill cucumbers, finely dice the red onions, dice the tomatoes, shred the cabbage and deseed and dice the chillies. Place all the vegetables in a bowl, squeeze over the citrus juices, sprinkle with salt and stir well. Chill for up to 3 days before serving.

3 cucumbers

6 pickled dill cucumbers

2 red onions

500 g/1 lb plum tomatoes

¼ white cabbage

2 serrano chillies, or 1 Thai

juice of 3 oranges

juice of ½ pink grapefruit

juice of 2 limes

1 tablespoon salt

Serves 8

Avocado relish

Avocados are packed with nutrients and their smooth, creamy texture is ideal for salsas.

Roast or grill the chillies and pepper, until the skins are blackened and blistered. Wrap in clingfilm for 3–5 minutes. Remove and discard the skin, cores and seeds, then chop the flesh into small pieces. Chop the avocados and brush with lemon juice. Place in a bowl, add the pepper and chillies, then stir in the spring onions, coriander and vinegar. Serve as a relish or as a dip with tortillas.

2 green chillies

1 red pepper

2 ripe avocados, halved and peeled

juice of 1 lemon

4 spring onions, finely chopped

1 large bunch of coriander, roughly chopped

125 ml/4 fl oz vinegar

Serves 4

Green chilli paste

A mixture of fresh and roasted chillies make a paste that's perfect used like mustard with dishes such as roasted chicken or grilled tuna steaks.

Roast or grill the Anaheim chillies until the skins are blackened and blistered. Wrap in clingfilm for 3–5 minutes. Remove and discard the skin, cores and seeds, then chop the flesh into small pieces. Place in a blender or food processor with the habaneros and garlic and purée to a paste.

4 Anaheim chillies

2 habanero chillies, cored and deseeded

1 garlic clove, crushed

Makes 1 jar, about 125 g/4 oz

Green chilli corn muffins
with chilli and lime butter

Chilli powder and fresh chillies give these
muffins lots of bite – for even more spice,
serve with this chilli and lime butter. This is
a quick and easy recipe – just 10 minutes to
prepare and 12–15 minutes to cook.

To make the muffins, sieve the flour, polenta, baking
powder and chilli powder together into a mixing
bowl. In a separate bowl, mix the milk, melted butter,
and beaten eggs, then fold into the dry mixture. Stir
in the grated orange rind and the chopped chillies.
Spoon the batter into a buttered 12-muffin pan and
bake in a preheated oven at 400°F (200°C) Gas
Mark 6 for about 12–15 minutes until firm.
Remove and set aside on a wire rack.
To make the chilli and lime butter, beat all the
ingredients together until soft and creamy.
Serve with the warm muffins.

250 g/8 oz plain flour

250 g/8 oz fine polenta

3 teaspoons
baking powder

1 tablespoon
mild chilli powder

175 ml/6 fl oz milk

75 g/3 oz butter, melted

2 medium-sized eggs,
lightly beaten

grated rind of 1 orange

2 green chillies,
deseeded and chopped

**chilli and
lime butter**

grated rind of 1 lime

50 g/2 oz butter

pinch of chilli powder

Makes 12

chillies are a **surprising**, zippy

addition to these buttery yellow muffins

Index